WHEN A FRIEND DIES

Updated
3rd Edition

A BOOK FOR TEENS ABOUT GRIEVING & HEALING

Marilyn E. Gootman, Ed.D.

free spirit
PUBLISHING®

Library of Congress Cataloging-in-Publication Data
Names: Gootman, Marilyn E., author.
Title: When a friend dies : a book for teens about grieving and healing / Marilyn E. Gootman, Ed.D.
Description: Updated 3rd edition. | Minneapolis, MN : Free Spirit Publishing, [2019]
Identifiers: LCCN 2018058106 | ISBN 9781631984228 (pbk) | ISBN 9781631984235 (web pdf) | ISBN 9781631984242 (epub)
Subjects: LCSH: Grief in adolescence—Juvenile literature. | Bereavement in children—Juvenile literature. | Bereavement in adolescence—Juvenile literature. | Grief in children—Juvenile literature. | Teenagers and death—Juvenile literature. | Children and death—Juvenile literature.
Classification: LCC BF724.3.G73 G66 2019 | DDC 155.9/370835—dc23 LC record available at https://lccn.loc.gov/2018058106

The quotes from Nadia Morillo (p. 4), Alexis Gendron (p. 14), and Augustus Griffith Jr. (p. 18) are excerpted from the book *Parkland Speaks: Survivors from Marjory Stoneman Douglas Share Their Stories*, Sarah Lerner, ed. (New York: Crown Books for Young Readers, 2019).

Edited by Pamela Espeland and Alison Behnke
Cover and interior design by Shannon Pourciau

Printed in China 51497

Free Spirit Publishing
An imprint of Teacher Created Materials
9850 51st Avenue North, Suite 100
Minneapolis, MN 55442
(612) 338-2068
help4kids@freespirit.com
freespirit.com

FSC
www.fsc.org
MIX
Paper from
responsible sources
FSC® C155903

"A great starting place for young people who are hurting."

—*Voice of Youth Advocates*

"This compassionate book gracefully addresses the unique needs of teen grievers. It is accessible without being patronizing and allows them to work through their experience by building on the stories of others."

—Alan Wolfelt, Ph.D.,
director of the Center for Loss and Life Transition

"This compassionate, user-friendly book lists pages of resources and suggested reading, and should be made available to teens."

—*School Library Journal*

"*When a Friend Dies* offers a voice of understanding and guidance during the very personal and often lonely experience of loss. Dr. Gootman's book is a friend who shares our journey of grief, a friend who does not take offense if we just want to be alone, and a friend we can introduce to others who need comfort. I am truly grateful for this book."

—John Bell, singer/guitarist, Widespread Panic

To my children, Elissa, Jennifer, and Michael

This book was inspired by my love and compassion for you and your friends. While I cannot protect you from losses, I hope I can help you through them.

CONTENTS

FOREWORD

by Michael Stipe, singer/songwriter, R.E.M.

When a Friend Dies is a book about acceptance and compassion. Accepting the sadness, confusion, and pain we experience with loss is as important as healing and moving forward. Showing compassion for yourself is about letting the feelings come and go as they do naturally. There is no right or wrong way to feel when someone dies.

Right now, you may be feeling things you've never felt before—and if you can't understand what you're going through, how could anyone else? No one can completely understand. Everybody hurts in their own way, and your grieving and pain are uniquely your own. But feeling lonely and grieving on your own isn't the same as *being* alone. You're not alone.

In this book, other teens share how they felt when their friend died. Reading their words can give you a chance to reflect on your own feelings in a new way. The book's questions and suggestions offer help and reassurance that you can make it through. Be gentle with yourself, take the time you need, and know that the greatest tribute to your friend is just being *you*.

"I just can't believe this happened to one of us." —Seth

"I was at the mall and thought I saw her. When I got close and saw it wasn't her, I felt so sad." —Noor

"I can't believe she is gone. She was so young and alive." —Erica

"It seems like any minute he should walk into the room. It doesn't seem like he is really gone." —David

"It feels like an alarm clock is supposed to go off soon and this will all be over." —Tanisha

INTRODUCTION

Kids are not supposed to die. It's against all the rules of nature. It's not right. It's not fair. It shouldn't ever happen. But it does happen . . . and when it does, it's scary.

If someone you know has died, this book is for you. I hope it will bring you comfort and help you heal.

When my daughter Elissa was a teenager, one of her friends died. I saw how this death affected my daughter. I spent a lot of time talking with her and being with her, but I also wished there was a book I could give to her. At that time, most books written about death and dying spoke *about* teenagers, not *to* them. As you'll see, this book speaks directly to you.

Some of the words are mine. Some of the words are those of teenagers whose friends have died, or of famous people who have spoken or written about death. All are meant for you to read at your own pace, in your own time.

You might read this book from cover to cover all at once, starting now. You might read it in little pieces—a page or two today, a paragraph tomorrow, more the day after or next week. How you read it is up to you. But do try to think about the questions, because they will help you understand what is happening to you. And do try the suggestions—some of them or all of them. They have helped other teenagers, and they may help you too. You won't know unless you give them a chance.

If you think you need more help, consider talking with a counselor or a therapist. You're going through a lot right now—maybe more than you can handle on your own, or with this book, or even with the support of parents, other family members, or close friends. Counselors and therapists are trained to help people through tough times. On pages 102–105, you'll find ideas about where to start looking for this kind of expert help.

You may want to read more books about death and dying. You'll find a list of possibilities on pages 118–119. You can also ask a librarian for ideas, or the media specialist at your school, a school counselor, a religious or spiritual leader, or anyone else whose advice you value and trust.

Bottom line? *You should do whatever works for you to help yourself heal.* You have had a terrible shock, and you need to take care of yourself.

This book can be a part of taking care of yourself. Share it with family adults and teachers. They need to know what you are going through, and this book may help them understand. Especially if you sometimes have trouble putting your feelings into words, this book can speak for you.

Whatever you decide to do—about this book, about your grief, about anything in your life right now—I can promise you one thing: *You will heal with time.* You have probably heard this before. Maybe you don't believe it, but it's true. Not because I say so—because other teenagers say so. They have lived through, learned from, and grown by the horrible experience of having a friend die. You can too.

Marilyn Gootman
Athens, Georgia

"This whole experience has made me look at things differently. I will not take anything for granted." —Nadia Morillo

"How can life ever be the same?" —Omar

"Will I ever feel okay again?" —Tomas

"When my friend died, the rest of the world kept going. I wanted the world to stop and I wanted to just scream out, 'Doesn't anyone realize that I am hurt?' I kept looking at people and thinking, 'You don't have a care, and look at me, one of my friends just died.'" —Selina

HOW CAN I STAND THE PAIN?

Shock, terror, and disbelief may bombard your body and mind when a friend dies. Surely it must be a mistake! How can it be—alive and breathing one minute, and gone the next?

The pain may seem unbearable. You may fear that your mind is on overload. You might even worry that you'll go insane.

Don't panic! You won't always feel this bad. The pain will lessen as time goes on.

After a while, your sad feelings will become fewer and farther between, and your happy feelings will return. Death gashes emotions, just like a knife gashes skin. With time and care, both kinds of wounds heal. They leave scars, but they do heal.

Try to be gentle with yourself. When things start to feel unbearably painful, find a healthy, caring, loving way to distract yourself.

"Caring for myself is not self-indulgence, it is self-preservation."

—AUDRE LORDE

You don't have to do all your grieving at once.

What activities soothe you and keep your mind occupied when you feel overwhelmed?

It's okay to take your mind off your grieving for a while. Listen to music, write, draw, make something, exercise . . .

"I cried hysterically, and then I went numb—kind of like I was watching myself from the outside." —Nicole

"I can't feel anything. It doesn't feel real." —Devin

"It's easy to convince yourself it's just a bad joke or a dream." —Théo

WHY CAN'T I FEEL ANYTHING?

You may be too stunned to feel anything. You may feel like you're living in a dream.

There is nothing wrong with you. Sometimes people's minds close down when they feel overwhelmed. They shut out the reality of what has happened. This is your mind's way of protecting you from feeling overloaded with pain.

Give yourself some time to let your feelings surface. Then, when they're ready to come out, let them.

"One must go through periods of numbness that are harder to bear than grief."

—ANNE MORROW LINDBERGH

"The first day back to school was a bitter taste of reality, when you notice the absence. Even after the funeral I still in a way expected her to be there, like it was all a bad dream." —Shanda

"Don't tell me to get over it already!" —Nicholas

"I've come to realize that grief is something beyond one's control. Something else takes over like an involuntary muscle, working its way through the tragedy." —Amy

HOW LONG WILL THIS LAST?

Dealing with death takes time—not just days, but weeks, months, and maybe even years.

You won't be sad and gloomy for the rest of your life. You won't always feel as bad as you do now. Grieving comes and goes. Sometimes you'll feel down, and sometimes you won't.

Nature has an amazing way of giving your mind and body a break from your hurt once in a while. You may feel sad, then be fine for a few months, then experience sadness and loss again at a later time. This cycle may repeat itself many times during your life.

There's no set schedule for grief. When you feel like grieving, then that is the right time for you. If you let yourself grieve instead of locking your grief inside, the hurt will get smaller and smaller as time goes on. The wound will slowly close up, leaving a healed scar.

IS IT WRONG TO GO TO PARTIES AND HAVE FUN?

You have a right and a responsibility to enjoy life and get meaning out of it even though your friend has died. While you will have sad times, you are also entitled to laugh and have fun when you are in the mood.

You do not need to feel guilty because you are having fun when your friend is not. Staying sad all the time will not help you or your friend.

"You cannot prevent the birds of sorrow from flying over your head, but you can prevent them from building a nest in your hair."

—CHINESE PROVERB

What activities do you enjoy?

Do you have any special hobbies?

Is there an interest you have always wanted to explore?

Maybe now is the time to start.

"It seems like everyone is staring at me." —Mei

"Is there something wrong with me that I'm not crying?" —Jules

"Just because I seem okay on the outside doesn't mean I truly am." —Alexis Gendron

HOW SHOULD I BE ACTING?

There is no single right way to respond to death. Grief takes many forms. Each person's grief is unique.

Express your grief in the way that feels most real to you.

"Trust life, and it will teach you, in joy and sorrow, all you need to know."

—JAMES BALDWIN

"I'm too scared to cry."
—Maria

"There are times when I want to cry and can't." —Sam

"Today is the worst day of my life. I have been crying helplessly for hours." —Keisha

Crying

Some people sob and cry. Sadness wells up inside them and pours out.

Some people scream and wail. That can help them let out their tension.

Some people stay silent, sometimes crying by themselves, sometimes not.

Just because people are quiet and don't talk about what happened doesn't mean that they aren't hurting. Sometimes people are so shocked or scared that they can't cry. Sometimes they are ashamed of admitting their feelings to others. Sometimes they cry inside.

"Tears are the silent language of grief."
—VOLTAIRE

"I just want to stay in bed and sleep all day and not have to think about it." —Eli

"Sleep is my only escape."
—Augustus Griffith Jr.

"I can't sleep at night. I just keep going over the details in my mind, over and over." —Joel

Sleeping

Some people go to bed and wake up at their usual times. They get a good night's sleep. Their minds are able to take a break from the pain.

Some people sleep much more than usual. Maybe sleep helps them escape the pain, or maybe sleep comes because they are so tired from sadness and mourning.

Grieving takes a huge amount of energy from both your mind and your body. You can expect to feel tired.

Some people can hardly sleep at all. Nightmares and scary thoughts might keep invading their minds. Or they might not be able to sit or lie still. Maybe moving around helps them avoid painful thoughts that are more than they can stand.

Going without enough sleep can make you moodier and more sensitive. It can affect your performance at school, in sports, and in other activities. It can make you look tired and feel irritable. Eventually, it can make you sick.

Try to sleep, even if you don't want to and even if you're sure that you couldn't possibly sleep anyhow. Here are some ideas that might help you get to sleep:

- Exercise earlier rather than later in the day.

- Relax for an hour or two before going to bed. Read a light, funny book, or listen to soothing music or something humorous or entertaining. Take a hot shower or bath.

- If you're comfortable with it, take a break from your phone, tablet, or computer before bed. The light from these screens can make it harder to fall asleep, and the things you read online might also make it hard for your mind to rest.

- Avoid caffeine, nicotine, alcohol, and other drugs.

- Cut back on sweets.

- Drink a glass of warm milk or a cup of caffeine-free tea like chamomile or mint.

- Eat a light snack before bed—a banana, popcorn, toast and jam, nuts, a kiwi, or some other healthy food with some carbohydrates.

Eating

Some people eat like they usually do. Their bodies keep going like always. For them, eating is a habit that doesn't change.

Some people stop eating. The thought of food turns them off. They may forget to eat. Sometimes their insides are so tied up in knots that it hurts to eat. Or they may vomit when they eat.

Some people overeat. Food, especially sweets and other high-calorie, high-fat junk foods, can seem comforting at times like these.

f you're not hungry, try to eat something anyway. The last thing you need right now is to starve yourself. Losing weight because you're too sad to eat is not healthy. Especially during times of stress, you need energy to function.

If you really, truly can't eat a bite, or if you can't seem to *stop* eating, talk to an adult you trust.

Have your eating patterns changed?

Think about what you are eating. Try to choose foods that are tasty and are also good for you.

Eating too many sweets may make you feel better for a short time, but the "sugar crash" that follows will make you feel worse.

WILL I BE CHANGED?

As time goes on, some people begin to act like they used to. They do not seem to be changed by the experience of having a friend die. They may feel changed on the inside but not show it on the outside.

Some people become silly and giddy. They may joke and fool around a lot because of the tension they feel. They hurt, even if it doesn't look that way.

Some people may become quiet and very sad. They may not want to be "cheered up," but they may want to talk.

"I can be changed by what happens to me. I refuse to be reduced by it."

—MAYA ANGELOU

Do you think you have changed?
If so, how?

Do you think people are treating
you differently now?

If so, how do you feel
when that happens?

WHAT IS "NORMAL"?

All these ways of reacting to the death of a friend or someone you know are "normal."

Don't judge yourself or others by the way you act or the way they act. Pain is pain, no matter how it looks on the outside.

Don't waste your time comparing one person's reactions to another's, or one person's pain to another's. Everyone hurts, and everyone has the right to express that pain in their own way.

Before your friend died, you may have thought that all people grieve by crying. Now you know that this isn't true for everyone. Sometimes you can clearly see another person's sadness. Sometimes you can't see it at all. And sometimes people camouflage their true feelings. They may act carefree or boisterous, even though they are hurting inside.

WHAT IF I HARDLY KNEW THE PERSON?

You don't have to be a person's best friend to feel the pain of grief when they die. If you just knew *about* the person, you may feel pain. You may even feel pain if you hear about, read about, or watch a news report about a complete stranger who has died.

You may be reminded of other losses you experienced earlier in your life. You may be frightened by the realization that if this person died, you could die too. You may have liked or admired the person, even though you didn't know them well or at all.

You have the right to your pain. Don't compare it to the pain of someone else who knew the person better. *Pain is pain.*

"I wasn't even there. I didn't even know any of the victims. So why am I so upset?" —Miguel

"Sometimes, when I learn about a horrible tragedy, I feel guilty that I'm glad I wasn't there." —Jamil

"I feel out of place because I didn't know him, but I still feel sad." —Leni

When a disaster or tragedy occurs—whether it's close to home or far away—TV and the internet can make it seem like we are there. We are not present in person, but we are "there."

We empathize with others who have lost loved ones. We ache with compassion for them. We feel our own grief and deep sadness for what has happened. We fear that the same thing could happen to us. Suddenly, the world seems like a very unsafe place.

Feeling the pain of others and empathizing with them is a virtue, not a weakness. Fearing that the same thing could happen to us is normal, not self-centered.

"The only whole heart is a broken one."
—THE KOTZKER REBBE

Try not to focus on negative images of tragedy and suffering. Instead, work on filling your mind with positive images. Think about the courageous, caring people who are helping others. Think about happier times in your own life.

Play with a pet, watch a funny movie, get involved in a project, give yourself a treat, or try some relaxation techniques like taking slow, deep breaths. Make a list of things you've done to get through other difficult situations. Choose one or more to try again.

Thinking about or looking at real-life images of a tragedy can make your pain worse. Protect yourself by trying not to let those pictures into your mind, including things you saw in person and also images you've seen in the news or online. Instead, while it may be hard, try to replace those pictures with positive images of your friend or fun times you had together. Steer your mind to focus on these positive ideas and thoughts.

HOW CAN I HANDLE MY FEELINGS?

Many thoughts pass through people's minds when they are grieving. These thoughts often trigger strong feelings. Facing and understanding these feelings will help you heal.

"Why did my friend have to die? She was so pretty and smart and nice." —Penny

"I was sitting in class with her just yesterday. In two years when we graduate, she won't be there." —Beth

"Why did he choose to leave us behind?" —Ken

Why did my friend have to die?

You may feel like screaming this question out loud to the sky. Maybe your friend died from an illness or an overdose, was killed in an accident, was murdered, or took their own life. Those are all causes of death. But none of them answers the question, "Why?"

People, faiths, and cultures have many ways of answering this question. You may find that one of these answers comforts you. You may come up with your own answer. Or you may keep searching for an answer that makes sense to you.

"You don't get to choose how you're going to die. Or when. You can only decide how you're going to live. Now."

—JOAN BAEZ

"If only she hadn't gone to pick up her boyfriend at the airport." —Ruth

"If only we had left a few minutes later." —DeShawn

"If only I had taken away his keys." —Andrew

If only . . .

"If only I had done . . ."

"If only I had said . . ."

"If only . . ."

These are thoughts that torment many people when someone dies. The truth is that awful things happen, and often nobody can stop them.

Death is scary. It makes us feel powerless. Feeling guilty is a way to avoid feeling powerless. But you are not guilty if your friend has died. It isn't fair to expect yourself to stop another person's death. Nor could you hasten another person's death through your understandable wishes that their pain would end.

"No willpower could prevent someone's dying."

—ANNIE DILLARD

"If only I had been friendlier to her." —Tamika

"If I had been there, maybe I could have done something to stop him." —Connor

"I never told her how much I cared about her. If only she had known, she might not have killed herself." —Felicia

f your friend died in an accident, through murder or other violence, from an overdose, or from an illness, then your "if onlys" are your mind's way of helping you feel some control in your life at a very out-of-control time.

If your friend died by suicide, it was your friend's decision, not yours. You are not responsible for that decision. You could not control your friend's thoughts or actions any more than someone else can control yours.

Almost all suicide survivors (that is what people are called who are still alive after someone they care about dies by suicide) blame themselves. But no one is to *blame* for a suicide, not even the person who died. However, that person is *responsible* for their own death.

Calling a person responsible is not the same as blaming. It's just stating a fact.

Almost all suicide survivors wonder, "Why did the person choose to leave me?" It's normal to feel abandoned or rejected. When people take their own lives, their primary goal is to end their pain. They do not choose to leave *us*. They choose to leave their pain. They are not thinking rationally.

They may even believe that their loved ones will be better off without them. They are mistaken.

Sometimes it's hard to think of the happy memories when someone dies by suicide. Try not to let that final act rob you of your good times together.

Try not to think about how your friend died. Focus instead on how your friend *lived*.

"I wish I had listened to him. I should have done something." —Terrell

"I feel guilty because she was sick for so long that I was secretly hoping she would die already." —Cari

"I wish I had told her not to go." —Jessica

I wish . . .

"I wish I had been nicer to my friend . . ."

"I wish we hadn't argued . . ."

"I wish I could take back what I said . . ."

This is another way guilt shows its ugly face. The truth is that arguments, fights, and anger are all part of normal living and feeling. Nobody is perfect, not even the person who died.

"Guilt is perhaps the most painful companion of death."

—ELISABETH KÜBLER-ROSS

Life would be very boring if we all tiptoed around each other, afraid to ever disagree or be angry because we thought another person might die soon. What went on before has nothing to do with your friend's death.

t is very unlikely that you could have done anything to stop your friend's death. Instead of feeling guilty, try helping another person.

Do something kind and thoughtful for someone else. This is the best way to get back some of the power you have lost.

"Making meaning of what happened, making the world a better place to counteract the bad: That is resilience."

—DR. RACHEL YEHUDA

"When I was in sixth grade my best friend was killed in a car accident . . . I can remember how our class acted the next day at school. No one was allowed to touch her desk—a rule someone in our class made. It was almost like a shrine." —Carla

Sometimes people are afraid to say anything bad about someone who has died. They turn the dead person into a saint.

Every person in this world has strong points and weak points, including those who have died. Loving someone means being honest and accepting the whole person, both the good and the bad, even if the person is dead.

"I'm just numb. I can't study or be with friends or do anything." —Enrico

"I don't know what to do. I can't seem to focus on anything." —Amira

"All I do is sit and stare into space." —Matthew

I can't think!

The shock of a sudden death can leave some people feeling as if their minds are frozen. This may be nature's way of protecting your mind so that everything can sink in more slowly and you won't be so overwhelmed.

Talking to others and sharing your sadness will help your mind slowly begin to thaw. As it does, you will start to adjust to your loss.

Sometimes it may seem easier to stay frozen and deny that you are bothered by what happened. But denying something will not make it go away. Denying your feelings will only keep your pain locked inside where it cannot be healed.

"Between grief and nothing,
I will take grief."

—WILLIAM FAULKNER

When a friend dies, it has to hurt. Try to admit this to yourself, and talk to someone who will listen and understand.

"Everyone says that my friend is in 'a better place.' How the hell do they know?" —Logan

"It's not fair! They didn't deserve to die. How could he have killed them?" —Val

"There are so many bad people in the world. She was one of the good ones. Why did she have to die?" —Alexis W.

"First my grandfather died, and then a month later my best friend was accidentally killed. What does God have against me?" —Patrick

I'm so angry!

You may feel red-hot anger when a friend dies. You may want to blame someone for your friend's death—another person, your friend's parents, a boyfriend or girlfriend, or God. And, of course, it makes sense that you would be furious if someone killed your friend.

You might even be angry at your friend for dying—for being careless, for getting sick, for not wearing a seatbelt, for drinking, for taking their own life, or just for leaving you.

You have a right to be angry. It is not fair that your friend has died—not for your friend, and not for you. Go ahead and feel angry. But be careful not to turn your anger onto yourself or others. Be sure to get your anger out in a way that will not hurt anyone.

"Holding on to anger is like grasping a hot coal."

—BUDDHA

Run, work out, or go to a place where you can yell at the top of your lungs. Try to think of constructive ways to use the energy from your anger. Build something. Create something.

Do whatever you can to release some of your anger without hurting yourself or others. Most important, talk about it.

Or you can use the energy of your anger to make the world a better place. Here are some ideas. See pages 115–117 to help you get started.

- Form a Students Against Destructive Decisions chapter at your school.

- Start a seatbelt campaign in your school or community.

- Advocate for gun safety.

- Address climate change.

- Speak up for the equality of all people, regardless of gender identity, sexuality, race, or religion.

- Register to vote and work to get other young adults to register to vote.

- Do a random act of kindness.

- Volunteer to help others.

- Take positive action in a way that makes sense to you.

"Turn your wounds into wisdom."
—OPRAH WINFREY

What would help you release your anger and calm down?

"People are always acting sympathetic and saying they know how I feel, but they don't know how I feel." —Brittany

I feel so alone.

It is normal to feel lonely and left behind after a friend dies. The death has ripped a hole in your life. Your friend is gone, and now it seems as if you must work it out alone.

But you are not alone. Reach out to other people, including those you may not have been friendly with in the past. Try to share your pain. If the people you talk to knew your friend, they may be suffering too. By sharing your pain with each other, you will all begin to heal.

Talk to your parents, if you can. If you can't, try to find other adults who can listen—counselors, teachers, other relatives, family friends, neighbors, your friends' families, coaches, youth group leaders, religious or spiritual leaders.

If you know the parents or family of the person who died, try talking with them. Share fond memories of your friend. They may appreciate it more than you will ever know.

"When we can talk about our feelings, they can become less overwhelming, less upsetting, and less scary. The people we trust with that important talk can help us know that we're not alone."

—FRED ROGERS

You may feel alone and left behind, but you are not alone. You have a whole community around you that shares your loss.

"When my best friend was killed, my mom went to the viewing and told me how she looked and I did not want to go. I wanted to remember her alive and beautiful. I did go to the funeral. This was a way for me to realize it was real. I felt like I was there but not really. My mind did not want to accept it. My family did a lot to help me by talking to me." —Nick

s there someone you would feel comfortable talking to? What about an adult you trust—a relative, a teacher, a school counselor? Or another person your age who also knew your friend who died?

Try to approach this person and begin to chat about anything—the weather, sports, school, a popular movie . . . Don't feel as if you have to start talking about your friend's death right away. Let the conversation come around to it. The other person may want to talk about it as much as you do.

Consider joining a support group. A support group is a group of people who share problems and feelings similar to yours. They meet regularly with a counselor or a therapist and talk together.

Support groups can be very helpful, especially for people who are grieving. Knowing that others are experiencing thoughts and reactions like yours, and being with people who reach out and support each other, can help you heal.

Sometimes support groups are available in schools, especially when a student has died. If your school doesn't offer support groups, check with a counselor or therapist, social worker, or mental health agency. See pages 103–105 for ways to do this. Someone will help you find a group that is right for you. Keep trying.

I'm afraid to get close to someone else. What if that person dies too?

The pain of losing a friend can be excruciating. It makes sense to want to avoid ever feeling such pain again. But cutting yourself off from other people because you're afraid of losing them will only make your pain worse by increasing your loneliness.

Of course, there is no guarantee that another friend will not die, even if it is unlikely. But there *is* a guarantee that reaching out to friends can ease your pain and help you through this difficult time.

"If you're going through hell, just keep going."

—WINSTON CHURCHILL

Needing a friend at this time is a tribute to your friend who died. After all, your friend helped you realize the importance of friendship.

Look around. Do you see anybody who might be an interesting friend?

"My best friend was shot and killed. We were best friends since I was four years old. Now I feel angry all the time. I even got mad at a friend who came over to see me. It's like I don't want a friend anymore." —Daryl

If I get close to other people, am I betraying my friend who died?

Some people think that if they make new friends, they are not being loyal to the friend who died. They go out of their way to avoid new friendships.

This doesn't help you, and it doesn't help your friend who died. You can stay loyal to your friend and still reach out to others—including brand-new friends. Your friend who died will always remain in your heart and in your mind.

"Friendship doubles our joy and divides our grief."

—SWEDISH PROVERB

"We don't feel close like a group anymore. The guys won't come over and be with us." —Marisa

"Some of us want to talk about our friend who died. Some of us don't want to talk about it. We used to get along, but now things are weird." —Tyrell

Some of my friends have changed. I feel like I have lost them too.

People react in various ways when someone dies. Some may need to break away from painful reminders of the friend they have lost. These reminders might include friends they shared in common. Others may be so very sad that they just don't seem the same. Either way, this may feel like another loss to you.

As you open up and talk to people, you may find yourself making new friends and also slowly returning to feeling close to your old friends.

"

"After my friend died, I began to worry that my parents would die or that I might die." —Carlos

"The fire alarm went off and everyone froze." —Jia

"Every time a car backfires, I think it's a gun." —Anthony

"I dreamt there was a shooting at my school." —Evan

"I'm afraid a plane will crash into our house, or a bomb will go off in our town." —Ashley

"

I feel afraid all the time.

Sometimes you may feel like you'll go out of your mind thinking about what happened. The fact that death is so final is frightening not just for you, but for all of us. Close your mind down for a while if you have to. It's okay to blank out the scary thoughts to give your mind a rest.

It makes sense to be afraid after a sudden, horrifying event like a shooting, terrorist attack, or natural disaster. Try not to let that fear overwhelm you. Instead, try to process it by talking with others. Although it may not seem like it right now, events like these are the exception, not the norm.

Your school probably is more prepared to protect you than you may think. If you feel comfortable doing so, talk to teachers and administrators about your worries. Open up a dialogue. Keep the lines of communication open so that you can let them know your concerns and they can let you know what they are doing to keep everyone safe.

> "Death is not the enemy; living in constant fear of it is."
> —NORMAN COUSINS

Sometimes it may be hard to stop thinking about your friend and what happened. Disturbing thoughts may come into your mind, even when you're enjoying yourself. This happens to many people.

Sometimes people feel guilty about having fun. They think sad thoughts on purpose so they won't enjoy themselves.

"You can clutch the past so tightly to your chest that it leaves your arms too full to embrace the present."

—JAN GLIDEWELL

You have a right and a responsibility to live your life and to enjoy it as much as you can.

You cannot help your friend by holding yourself back from living your own life to the fullest.

Call a friend, go for a walk, watch a movie, or take deep breaths.

What works for you?

If you feel overwhelmed, take a break. Think of a way to escape from your thoughts and feelings.

"One minute everything is fine, and a few seconds later I want to break down and cry." —Megan

"Every time I hear that song, I'm afraid someone else will die." —Jesse

"In the car on the way to the funeral, my mind became flooded with memories. Slowly at first the scenes appeared in my mind's eye and then built up to frantic speeds." —Anna

All of a sudden it hits me, and I get sad.

Sometimes you may find that certain situations—hearing a certain song on the radio, being in a certain place, a change in the weather, words, a smell, a photo you see online, a birthday or holiday gathering—remind you of your friend. They may even remind you of when and how your friend died.

When this happens, you may become very sad, anxious, or even panicky. Your heart may start racing and your breathing may speed up. Or your mind may go blank and you may feel numb all over.

"Sorrow was like the wind. It came in gusts."

—MARJORIE KINNAN RAWLINGS

This happens to so many people who have lost someone in a sudden, shocking way that it has a name: post-traumatic stress disorder, or PTSD.

PTSD can take many forms: for example, nightmares, pictures in your mind of your friend's death, flash-backs, fear that someone else close to you will die, painful sadness, trouble sleeping or concentrating, or feeling jumpy or anxious. You can experience PTSD whenever something reminds you of when and how your friend died.

You're not alone. Millions of people experience PTSD. Knowing about it can help you cope with it.

- Practice ways to relax so you can use one the next time you have these feelings. Do some deep breathing or stretching exercises. Tense every muscle in your body, then relax each one, starting with your head and working down to your toes—or starting with your toes and working up to your head.

- Learn how to meditate. Look online for resources or see if your community offers meditation classes.

- Replace unpleasant, frightening thoughts or images with positive ones. Try to "switch channels" in your mind to see a positive memory.

- Get some exercise every day, if you don't already. Walk, run, swim, lift weights—whatever you like to do.

- Talk with an adult you trust. Explain that you're having these feelings whenever you're reminded of your friend's death.

- Call or text a helpline. See pages 110–111.

What if nothing seems to work? What if these feelings don't start to fade? What if you just can't seem to get past your friend's death? Then it's time to talk with a professional who can help you—a healthcare provider, a therapist, a spiritual advisor, or a counselor. See pages 102–105 for information on finding the right person to help you.

When the anniversary of a death comes, you may feel like you did when it first happened. But that doesn't mean you're still in the same place.

You have moved forward, even if it doesn't always seem that way to you. You won't have to start the whole grieving process again.

> "After my friend died, all I could think was, 'Be young, stay young, raise hell while young.'"
> —Roy

> "We're all going to die someday. I know that now for sure. So it doesn't really matter what I do." —Jaime

I'd better enjoy myself as much as I can now, because who knows what tomorrow may bring?

Yes, you should enjoy your life every day. You can do this by living a full life and doing things you enjoy that make you feel worthwhile—things that give your life meaning.

But it is foolish and reckless to do self-destructive things—such as drinking, using drugs, smoking or vaping, or driving too fast—because you figure you should enjoy yourself now, while you have the chance.

Why run the risk of destroying your life? If you live a long life, and you probably will, won't this attitude hurt you in the long run?

Some people think that when a friend dies, this reduces the chances that something bad will happen to them. It's as if one death in a group of friends somehow "protects" the other friends from harm.

Statistically, your chances of dying are not any lower—or any higher—now than they were before your friend died. That is why you should still take good care of yourself. Risky behaviors are still risky behaviors.

How many ways can you have fun without hurting or endangering yourself or others?

Adults are hovering over me and smothering me.

Most people want to shield their loved ones from hurt. Few things hurt more than the death of a friend, so it's no wonder that adults are extra attentive or extra protective at times like these.

If someone is hovering, know that it's because they care. And know that it's okay to wish they would back off! Parents and other adults can't protect you from all the hurt in the world—and they shouldn't try. You need to learn to handle some hurt yourself.

Don't feel guilty about wanting your own space. But try to tell people kindly, without being harsh or rude. Remember that your friend's death has scared them too. Of course they want to hold you close; the idea that someone could lose a loved one has become all too real for them. They may be afraid of losing *you*.

Here are some things you may want to tell adults, especially those you live with who care for you (such as parents, stepparents, guardians, or foster parents):

- "I love you, and I know that you love me."

- "I understand that you are worried about me because of what has happened."

- "I need to deal with this. Please don't try to protect me."

- "Please don't tell me how to feel."

- "When I talk to you about my feelings, I'd appreciate it if you just listened."

- "Sometimes I might not want to talk to you. I might want to talk to my friends instead. They are going through the same thing I'm going through. We understand each other."

- "Sometimes I may want to talk to another adult I know—a teacher, counselor, or religious leader. This doesn't mean that I'm rejecting you. It just means I want to talk to someone who isn't so close to me."

On pages 118–119 you'll find a list of books that can help you better understand what you're going through and why. You may want to share this list—along with this book—with your family or others. Maybe they will want to read these books too.

HOW CAN I DEAL WITH MY GRIEF?

Healing any wound, in the body or the mind, takes time. Allow yourself that time. You are entitled to it.

Give yourself permission to grieve. Allow yourself to grieve when and where you need to.

Share your feelings. Write about them. Draw them. Talk to others about your feelings.

"If art can help us grieve, can help us mourn, then lean on it."

—LIN-MANUEL MIRANDA

Even though you may feel sad when you talk about your friend, talking will help your pain get smaller. Not talking won't make your pain go away. In fact, it may make it stronger. As you force your pain to stay inside, it pushes against you, trying to get out.

That's why it's so important to find someone—a friend or an adult—to talk to. Sharing your feelings with others is a healthy way to release some of your pain.

Sometimes when people don't take time to grieve, they become very angry. Often, they explode at other people and situations that have nothing to do with the death that they're grieving.

Try to think of your emotions inside you as steam inside a pipe. Just as a steam valve slowly releases steam so the pipe won't burst, you can set aside time to slowly grieve so your emotions won't spill out unpredictably or harmfully.

"Grief is not a disorder, a disease, or a sign of weakness. It is an emotional, physical, and spiritual necessity, the price you pay for love. The only cure for grief is to grieve."

—EARL GROLLMAN

If you allow yourself to grieve, you will eventually be able to temporarily set aside your grief at certain times. This may be particularly helpful when you really need to concentrate and cannot be distracted, such as during a test. Later, when you are ready, you can come back to your grief.

Remember to live your life to the fullest. Try to think of something positive you learned from your friend, something funny that happened when you were together, or a pleasant time you shared. Know that a part of your friend will always remain with you, because memories of your friend live on in your mind.

"Memories have to be our
most painful blessing."

—KANYE WEST

"When looking back on your lost loved one, try to picture them at their healthiest and happiest." —Theresa

What are your favorite
memories of your friend?

HOW CAN I HELP MYSELF HEAL?

Share, talk with others, write, draw, listen to music, write music, cuddle with a pet or a stuffed animal, or plant a tree in memory of your friend.

Visit your friend's family. It might be hard to see them, but you can help each other.

Many people find that reaching out to others, doing acts of kindness, and making the world a better place can help them heal from the death of a friend. For some ideas, see pages 54 and 115–117.

"What you do makes a difference,
and you have to decide what kind of
difference you want to make."

—JANE GOODALL

How can you translate your pain into positive actions that would be a tribute to your friend?

What would be a good way to keep your friend's memory alive—a meaningful memorial to your friend?

WHAT IF I CAN'T HANDLE MY GRIEF ON MY OWN?

Many people who have experienced a great loss find it helpful to speak to someone who has been specially trained to guide people through grieving.

Speaking to a counselor or therapist (psychologist, psychiatrist, or social worker) when you have been hurt by death is no different from going to a medical doctor when you have a deep cut. Both kinds of professionals are trained to help people heal.

Your first visit to a counselor or therapist may feel a bit scary and embarrassing. But if the person is in tune with your hurt—if they are willing to listen to you and understand your point of view—you will soon feel relieved to have this person to talk to and the awkwardness will fade. Give it time.

f you need to speak to a counselor or a therapist after someone you know has died, you are not "sick." You have been injured by events beyond your control, and you are getting help for your injury. It's that simple.

"It's time to tell everyone who's dealing with a mental health issue that they're not alone, and that getting support and treatment isn't a sign of weakness, it's a sign of strength."

—MICHELLE OBAMA

WHAT IF MY FRIENDS START ACTING STRANGE?

Many people who have suffered a sudden, shocking loss could be helped by talking with a counselor or a therapist. In particular, teenagers who are behaving in unusual ways could probably use some guidance. Keep an eye out for friends who:

- drink and/or use other drugs to numb their pain
- stop eating or eat very little
- eat a lot and then force themselves to vomit
- suddenly start doing very poorly in school
- talk about wanting to give up and die
- give away treasured possessions
- take self-destructive or even life-threatening risks
- act very aggressive
- act angry at the whole world
- withdraw from friends and family
- lose interest in things they used to enjoy

Have you noticed any of these behaviors in a friend? If so, speak to a responsible, caring adult—the school counselor, a teacher, your friend's parent, your own parent or other family member, or a religious or spiritual leader so that person can find help for your friend.

No, you are not betraying your friend. You are being a true, loving friend. The right thing to do—the most caring thing to do—is to tell a responsible, caring adult. You can't solve your friend's problems on your own. That would be an unfair burden for you to carry all by yourself.

Read the list of behaviors on page 99 again. Have you noticed any of them in yourself? If so, please get the help you need and deserve.

"Life was meant to be lived . . .
One must never, for whatever reason,
turn his back on life."
—ELEANOR ROOSEVELT

What adult can you approach to discuss your friend . . . or yourself?

Who do you think would be a calm, attentive listener?

Who might know where to guide you to get the help you need?

HOW CAN I FIND A COUNSELOR OR A THERAPIST?

There are many ways to find the help you need for you or for a friend. If one way doesn't work for you, try another. Don't give up! Help *is* available.

Get a personal referral.

Do you know someone who goes to a counselor or a therapist? If you both feel comfortable talking about it, ask that person for the name of the counselor or therapist. Ask the person's opinion of the counselor or therapist. Has the experience of talking with this professional been helpful?

If you don't know of anyone who is seeing a counselor or a therapist, ask another person you trust for some suggestions. Good possibilities might include your school counselor, your school psychologist, a teacher, a doctor, or a leader in your faith community.

See what resources are available in your community.

Following are some ideas you can try when looking for counseling. You may want to ask an adult—a parent or other family adult, a teacher, or a school counselor—to help you, since this process can be intimidating. Just because someone has a title is no guarantee that they are the right person for you to see and talk to. An adult can help you find the right person. That person should have experience in working with teenagers and/or experience with grief work.

- Search online for "mental health services" or "therapists" and the name of your city or town. Or look in an online phone directory for terms such as "Mental Health Services," "Counselors," "Therapists," "Social Workers," "Psychologists," "Psychiatrists," or "Psychotherapy."

- Look in a paper phone book for the same terms. If you don't have a paper phone book at home, your local library will have one.

- If your family has health insurance, reach out to the company and ask for a list of providers of mental health services that would be covered by your insurance. You can also ask your healthcare provider to give you a referral.

- Contact one or more of the national organizations listed on pages 110–114 of this book. They will give you the names of counselors or therapists who belong to their organizations and who live in your area.

- Call one or more of the places you have found in your research and ask about making an appointment or getting a referral. Some help people on a sliding-scale fee basis, which means that you pay only as much as you can afford.

HOW CAN I TELL IF A COUNSELOR OR THERAPIST CAN HELP ME?

You have many choices when it comes to seeking help. Psychologists, psychiatrists, social workers, psychiatric nurses, certified mental health workers, many school counselors, and certain faith leaders are qualified to provide therapy. But only *you* can decide whether someone is qualified to be *your* counselor or therapist.

Here are some questions to ask yourself about someone you are considering:

- Does this person seem to understand my feelings?

- Has this person experienced the death of someone close to them? (This isn't essential, but it often helps.)

- Can this person listen without being judgmental?

- Am I comfortable being honest with this person?

- Does this person accept me in a way that helps me accept myself?

Remember: Counseling or therapy is meant to ease your pain. Only you can tell whether it is working for you. If one person doesn't seem to be helping, try someone else. Keep trying until you find someone who is right for you.

WILL I EVER BE OKAY AGAIN?

At first, when a friend dies, it's hard to imagine how life can go on . . . but it does. It's hard to imagine that things will ever go back to normal, or almost normal . . . but they will.

I wish this had never happened to you and your friend, but it did. There is nothing you can do to change what has happened, but there is much you can do to help yourself.

I have gone through what you are going through now. I know other young people whose friends have died. I can make this promise: You will grow from this tragedy. You will learn more about yourself and others. You will become more sensitive. Your view of the world will change.

No one would ever choose to grow because of the death of a friend. But now that it has happened to you, what can you do to make meaning out of your experience? Think about that in the weeks, months, and years ahead. You will find a way.

Meanwhile, you may take some comfort in the words of others who have spoken or written about death. Go back and read the quotations by famous people—Michelle Obama, William Faulkner, James Baldwin, Jane Goodall, and others—found throughout this book. If there is one that is especially inspiring or helpful to you, write it down on a piece of paper and carry it in your wallet or calendar, or make it into an image on your phone or computer so you can look at it often. Or create your own meaningful phrase, sentence, or poem. Share your words with a friend who is also grieving. Help each other.

> "I still miss those I loved who are no longer with me, but I find I am grateful for having loved them. The gratitude has finally conquered the loss."
>
> —RITA MAE BROWN

RESOURCES
Crisis hotlines

Crisis Text Line
In the United States, text HOME to 741741.
In Canada, text HOME to 686868.
crisistextline.org
The Crisis Text Line provides free crisis support 24-7. Everyone who texts is connected with a crisis counselor who has been trained to listen and to work with you to help cope with challenges. They can help with any kind of painful emotion with which you need support during a crisis.

National Suicide Prevention Lifeline
1-800-273-TALK (8255)
suicidepreventionlifeline.org
The National Suicide Prevention Lifeline is a national network of local crisis centers across the US. Available 24-7, they can put you in touch with trained telephone counselors who can provide free and confidential emotional support for people in suicidal crisis or emotional distress. In addition, their website offers information specifically for teens (under the "youth" section of the site), as well as people who are LGBTQ+, deaf or hard of hearing, loss survivors, disaster survivors, Native Americans, Spanish speakers, and attempt survivors.

Substance Abuse and Mental Health Services Administration (SAMHSA) National Helpline

1-800-662-HELP (4357)

samhsa.gov

SAMHSA provides a confidential, free, 24-7 information service in English and Spanish for individuals and family members facing mental and/or substance use disorders. SAMHSA staff members direct callers to federal, state, and local organizations dedicated to treating and preventing mental illness. On the website, click "Find Treatment" to find treatment in your area as well as hotline numbers.

Teen Line

1-800-TLC-TEEN (852-8336) or (310) 855-4673 (6 to 10 PM PST)

teenlineonline.org

Text TEEN to 839863 in the US or Canada (6 to 9 PM PST). Teen Line is a confidential hotline for teenagers that operates every evening. If you have a problem or just want to talk with another teen who understands, you can contact them by phone or text. On their website, Teen Line also offers message boards, email options, a free app, and other resources and information.

The Trevor Project

1-866-488-7386

Text START to 678678

thetrevorproject.org

The Trevor Project is the leading national organization providing crisis intervention and suicide prevention services to lesbian, gay, bisexual, transgender, queer, and questioning (LGBTQ) people under the age of 25. It provides trained counselors to offer support through talk, text, or online chat 24-7 for young people who are in crisis, feeling suicidal, or in need of a safe and judgment-free place to talk.

Referrals and other support

American Association of Suicidology (AAS)

202-237-2280

suicidology.org

The American Association of Suicidology works to understand and prevent suicide. Their mission is to promote the understanding and prevention of suicide and to support those who have been affected by it. If you have lost a loved one to suicide, at their website click on "suicide survivors" and then click on the "SOS Directory" for a list of support groups. You can also search the site for "SOS Handbook" to find a handbook for survivors of suicide.

American Foundation for Suicide Prevention

1-888-333-AFSP (2377)

afsp.org

The American Foundation for Suicide Prevention is dedicated to advancing knowledge about suicide and the ability to prevent it. They provide information and education about depression and suicide and suggest many ways to get involved in the suicide prevention effort in your community.

American Psychiatric Association (APA)

202-559-3900

psychiatry.org

A psychiatrist is a medical doctor who is trained to help people with emotional problems. If you are looking for a psychiatrist, go to the APA website, click on "patients & families," and then click on "find a psychiatrist."

American Psychological Association (APA)

1-800-374-2721

apa.org

A psychologist is a counselor who usually has received a doctoral degree from a university. Visit the Psychology Help Center section of the APA's website and click on "Find a Psychologist" to get a referral to a psychologist in the United States or Canada. If you live elsewhere, you can contact your national psychological association or a local mental health facility.

The Dougy Center

1-866-775-5683

dougy.org

The Dougy Center runs the National Center for Grieving Children and Families, which provides support and training locally, nationally, and internationally to individuals and organizations seeking to assist grieving children, teens, young adults, and their families. Contact them to learn about groups in your area. On the website, click on "Grief Resources" to find support programs, help for teens, tip sheets, and podcasts.

Help Starts Here

helpstartshere.org

Help Starts Here is run by the National Association of Social Workers. A clinical social worker has received advanced education and training to help people deal with emotional problems. Social workers care for people in every stage of life, from children to the elderly, and help them overcome life's most difficult challenges as well as the troubles of everyday living. They can also provide advice for finding the right therapist. On the website, click on "find a social worker" to find online directories.

Mourning Cloak

414-704-7640

mourningcloak.org

Mourning Cloak provides volunteer training for those who would like to start grief support groups as well as consultations for structuring peer support groups and consultations for schools regarding specific students who are grieving. The website has many valuable grief resources for people of all ages. In addition, one of this organization's cofounders is also the director of the Center for Loss and Life Transition (centerforloss.com), which is dedicated to helping people who are grieving and those who care for them.

National Board for Certified Counselors (NBCC)

336-547-0607

nbcc.org

The NBCC maintains a registry of people who hold an advanced degree with a focus on counseling and who have met national standards developed by counselors. To find a certified counselor, scroll down and click on "Counselor Find."

Option B

optionb.org

Option B is dedicated to helping people build resilience and strength in the face of hard times. On this website, you can read and share personal stories, join groups for solidarity and support, and find information from experts. You can also connect with people who understand and get information that can help.

Summer camps and other programs

Camp Erin

267-687-7724

elunanetwork.org/camps-programs/camp-erin

Through Camp Erin, young people ages 6 to 17 can attend a free weekend camp that combines fun camp activities with grief education and emotional support led by grief professionals and trained volunteers. Camp Erin is offered in every Major League Baseball city as well as additional locations across the US and Canada.

Camp Kita

207-358-0093

campkita.com

Camp Kita is a nonprofit summer bereavement camp based in Maine. It is open to young people ages 8 to 17 who are survivors of a loved one's suicide. The camp is made possible by volunteers, including medical and clinical professionals, and is free of charge.

Comfort Zone Camp

1-866-488-5679

comfortzonecamp.org

Comfort Zone Programs are free of charge and include activities and support groups for young people ages 5 to 25 who are grieving. Held year-round across the country, their primary locations are California, Massachusetts, New Jersey, and Virginia.

Experience Camp

1-833-226-7385

experience.camp

Experience Camps are for boys and girls whose parent, sibling, or primary caregiver has died. The camps offer a one-week program that helps build confidence, encourages laughter, and allows campers to navigate their grief through friendship, teamwork, athletics, and the common bond of loss. There is no charge for the camp.

Outward Bound

outwardbound.org

1-866-467-7651

Outward Bound programs are intended to provide respectful healing experiences in a wilderness environment. To learn more, visit the website and click on "programs" and then on "grieving teens."

Taking action

DoSomething.org

212-254-2390

dosomething.org

DoSomething.org is a digital platform for powering offline action. It works to mobilize young people in more than one hundred countries. Visit their website to sign up for a volunteer, social change, or civic action campaign to make real-world impact on a cause you care about.

Everytown for Gun Safety

everytown.org

Everytown is a movement working to end gun violence and build safer communities. To see information specifically for students, visit everytown.org/start-sda-group to learn more about creating or joining a Students Demand Action Group in your area.

Inspire U.S.

inspire-usa.org

This nonpartisan group supports high schools in planning and conducting student peer-to-peer voter registration activities and helping young people make a difference in their communities.

March for Our Lives

marchforourlives.com

Based on a 2018 student-led demonstration in support of tighter gun control, this organization's website lists weekly actions to get young people registered, educated, and ready to vote for their lives.

The Random Acts of Kindness Foundation

randomactsofkindness.org

This foundation inspires people to practice kindness and to "pass it on" to others. They provide free educational and community ideas, guidance, and other resources on their website.

SAVE (Students Against Violence Everywhere)

nationalsave.org

SAVE Promise Clubs work to protect people, schools, and communities from violence before it happens. Established and led by students, these groups give young people a chance to show their leadership, creativity, and passion.

Students Against Destructive Decisions (SADD)

sadd.org

Students Against Destructive Decisions (SADD), formerly known as Students Against Driving Drunk, can provide you with information about how to start a SADD chapter in your school. They can also help you make an action plan for activities and programs dealing with underage drinking, other drug use, impaired driving, and other destructive decisions.

Volunteer Match

volunteermatch.org

One way to heal yourself is by helping others. You can check out volunteer opportunities in your area on this organization's website by typing in your location and clicking on "Get Started."

RECOMMENDED READING

Grief One Day at a Time: 365 Meditations to Help You Heal After Loss by Alan Wolfelt, Ph.D. (Fort Collins, CO: Companion Press, 2016). The book provides small, one-day-at-a-time doses of guidance and healing. Each entry includes an inspiring or soothing quote followed by a short discussion of the day's theme.

Healing After Loss: Daily Meditations for Working Through Grief by Martha W. Hickman (New York: William Morrow Paperbacks, 1994). This book offers a year's worth of short readings for people who have lost a loved one.

Healing Your Grieving Heart for Teens: 100 Practical Ideas by Alan D. Wolfelt, Ph.D. (Fort Collins, CO: Companion Press, 2001). A grief counselor offers compassionate suggestions for dealing with the scary, often uncontrollable emotions that come up after you've lost someone. This book also has a companion journal, *The Healing Your Grieving Heart Journal for Teens*, with thought-provoking questions to help you heal.

I Will Remember You: What to Do When Someone You Love Dies: A Guidebook Through Grief for Teens by Laura Dower (New York: Scholastic Paperbacks, 2001). Thoughts and quotations from famous people, personal stories from real teens, and creative exercises help you move through your pain and sorrow.

No Time for Goodbyes: Coping with Sorrow, Anger, and Injustice After a Tragic Death by Janice Harris Lord (Burnsville, NC: Compassion Press, 2014). This classic guide includes comments from survivors as well as insights and information from the author.

A Teen's Simple Guide Through Grief by Alexis Cunningham (Carson, CA: Jalmar Press, 2001). The sadness and depression that come with grief can be overwhelming. This short, simple book offers suggestions for daily steps that can help you feel better.

When Will I Stop Hurting? Teens, Loss, and Grief by Edward Myers (Lanham, MD: Scarecrow Press, 2004). Stories from teens who have lost a family member, advice for reaching out to others, encouragement to help you through the grieving process, and warning signs for when grief leads to depression.

Resources for adults

Caring for Kids After Trauma, Disaster, and Death: A Guide for Parents and Professionals by New York University Child Study Center, preventionweb.net/files/1899_VL206101.pdf (2006). Published by NYU Child Study Center, this excellent resource for helping kids after trauma, disaster, and death is available for free online.

Helping Teens Cope with Death by The Dougy Center for Grieving Children and Families (Portland, OR: The Dougy Center, 2011). The Dougy Center for Grieving Children and Families is internationally renowned for its peer support groups and training efforts to help young people recover from loss. This book details the unique experience of teen grief and offers ways for caring adults to support adolescents throughout the grieving process.

How Do We Tell the Children? A Step-by-Step Guide for Helping Children and Teens Cope When Someone Dies by Dan Schaefer and Christine Lyons (New York: HarperCollins, 2010). Practical advice on how to explain death and console grieving children.
National Alliance for Grieving Children
1-866-432-1542
childrengrieve.org

The National Alliance for Grieving Children raises awareness about the needs of children and teens who are grieving a death and provides education and resources for anyone who supports them. It is a professional member organization that offers continuing education, peer networking, an Annual Symposium on Children's Grief, and the National Database of Children's Bereavement Support Programs.

The National Center for School Crisis and Bereavement (NCSCB)

1-877-536-2722
schoolcrisiscenter.org
The NCSCB at the USC Suzanne Dworak-Peck School of Social Work is dedicated to helping schools support their students through crisis and loss. They provide crisis response, education, training, advocacy, and research.

Shared Grief Project

sharedgrief.org
The Shared Grief Project shares stories of individuals who have experienced a major loss at an early age and have gone on to live healthy, happy, and successful lives.

INDEX

About the author

Marilyn E. Gootman, Ed.D., is founder of Gootman Education Associates, an educational consulting company that provides workshops and seminars for parents and educators focusing on successful strategies for raising and teaching children. Dr. Gootman has been in the  teaching profession for over 25 years, and her teaching experiences range from elementary school to the university level. The author of numerous books and articles, she is known nationally for her advocacy efforts on behalf of children, parents, and teachers. Her media appearances include CNN and other major networks, as well as radio and television broadcasts throughout the United States and Canada. Marilyn and her husband, Elliot, are the parents of three grown children, and they have seven grandchildren.